The magic key

A playscript
adapted from a story by
Roderick Hunt

by Jacquie Buttriss and Ann Callander

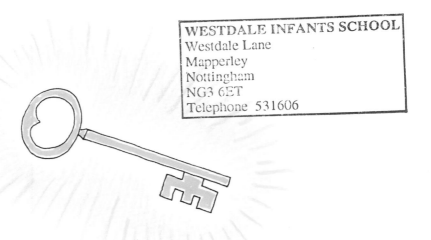

Characters

Narrator 1

Narrator 2

Chip

Biff

This play has four speaking parts so that it can be read aloud in small groups. Sound effects can be added by children when they are familiar with the playscript but they have not been written in.

Narrator 1

Narrator 2

Chip   **Biff**

Scene 1

Narrator 1 Scene 1   'The magic box'
The box was by Chip's bed.

Narrator 2 Something was glowing inside it.

Narrator 1 Chip looked at the box.

Chip It's magic.

Narrator 2 Chip ran into Biff's room.

Chip Biff. Look at the box.

Narrator 1 Biff and Chip looked at the box.

Chip Look! It's glowing.

Narrator 2 They opened the box and looked inside.

Biff It's magic.

Scene 2

Narrator 1 Scene 2   'The magic key'
A key was in the box.

Biff Look at the key.

Chip It's glowing.

Biff It's a magic key.

Narrator 2 Biff picked up the magic key and the magic began.

Scene 3

Narrator 1 Scene 3   'Smaller and smaller'
Biff and Chip got smaller and
smaller and smaller.

Biff Oh help!

Chip It's magic.

Biff Look at the room.

Chip Everything looks big.

Biff Look at my big slippers.

Narrator 1 Chip picked up a pencil.

Chip Look at this big pencil.

Narrator 2 Biff picked up a pin.

Biff Look at this big pin.

Scene 4

Narrator 1 Scene 4   'The house'
Biff and Chip looked at the house.

Chip Look at the house.

Biff It looks like a big house.

Narrator 2 The windows were glowing.

Chip It's magic.

Narrator 1 Biff went to the door.

Chip Open the door.

Narrator 2 Biff pushed and pushed, but she couldn't get in.

Narrator 1 They went to the window.

Biff Open the window.

Narrator 2 Chip pulled and pulled, but he couldn't get in.

Scene 5

Narrator 1 Scene 5 'Help'
Something was coming.

Chip Oh help!

Biff Pick up the pin.

Narrator 2 Chip picked up the pin.

Chip Look! It's a little mouse.

Narrator 1 Biff and Chip looked at the mouse.

Narrator 2 The mouse looked at Biff and Chip.

Narrator 1 The mouse ran away.

Scene 6

Narrator 2 Scene 6   'Bigger and bigger'
Something was glowing.

Biff It's the key.

Chip Pick it up.

Narrator 1 Biff and Chip got bigger and bigger and bigger.

Biff Oh no!

Chip Oh help!

Biff It's the magic.

Narrator 2 The magic was over.

Chip What an adventure!

The end

Printed in Hong Kong